Simple Outlines

Workbook

Trackable Progress

K-3 Short Compositions Practice Workbook 1 of 3

SherLynne Beach, SuccessFamilies

Simple Outlines Workbook

Trackable Progress

K-3 Short Compositions Practice Workbook 1 of 3

By SherLynne Beach, SuccessFamilies

Copyright 2015 SherLynne Beach and SuccessFamilies

ISBN-13: 978-1517107659

ISBN-10: 1517107652

Introduction

I created these Writing Workbooks to assist my children in becoming proficient writers. These workbooks can be used with any writing program.

There are three books in the series – Outline, Rough Draft & Edit, and Final Copy. Each book has enough room for 60 writing projects, one for each week of the year, plus a few extra.

As the homeschooling mom that I am, I found this system to be quite helpful...something a little more formal to keep writing a special and respected activity...no more lost drafts in odd notebooks scattered around the house!

I hope you enjoy these as we do!

Find more resources at our website: www.SuccessFamilies.com

Dedication

To my children's success, and your children's.

To my mother, dedicated editor, great parent and grandparent, wonderful friend.

To my husband...ibid, forever.

Table of Contents

Date	Title	Page
		8
		10
		12
		14
		16
		18
		20
		22
		24
		26
		28
		30
		32
		34
		36
		38
		40
		42
		44
		46

		48
		50
		52
		54
		56
		58
		60
		62
		64
		66
		68
		70
		72
		74
		76
		78
		80
		82
		84
		86
		88
		90
		92
		94

		96
		98
		100
		102
		104
		106
		108
		110
		112
		114
		116
		118
		120
		122
		124
		126
		128
		130
		132
		134
		136
		138
		140

Outline Instructions

- Read the chosen passage.

- Outline the passage one sentence at a time.

- Number each sentence

- Use no more than three key words

- You can use additional symbols.

- Then, using only the outline, retell the passage to someone.

- Move on to the next book –ROUGH DRAFT

Outline

DATE:_______________________________________

TITLE:______________________________________

Remember:

Number each new sentence you outline, Use up to 3 words, Use extra symbols

____

____

____

____

____

____

____

____

Outline

DATE:_______________________________________

TITLE:______________________________________

Remember:

Number each new sentence you outline, Use up to 3 words, Use extra symbols

____

____

____

____

____

____

____

____

Outline

DATE:____

TITLE:____

Remember:

Number each new sentence you outline, Use up to 3 words, Use extra symbols

____

____

____

____

____

____

____

____

Outline

DATE:_______________________________________

TITLE:______________________________________

Remember:

Number each new sentence you outline, Use up to 3 words, Use extra symbols

---

Outline

DATE:____

TITLE:____

Remember:

Number each new sentence you outline, Use up to 3 words, Use extra symbols

Outline

DATE:____

TITLE:____

Remember:

Number each new sentence you outline, Use up to 3 words, Use extra symbols

____

____

____

____

____

____

____

____

Outline

DATE:____

TITLE:____

Remember:

Number each new sentence you outline, Use up to 3 words, Use extra symbols

Outline

DATE:_______________________________________

TITLE:_______________________________________

Remember:

Number each new sentence you outline, Use up to 3 words, Use extra symbols

____

____

____

____

____

____

____

____

Outline

DATE:____

TITLE:____

Remember:

Number each new sentence you outline, Use up to 3 words, Use extra symbols

____

Outline

DATE:____

TITLE:____

Remember:

Number each new sentence you outline, Use up to 3 words, Use extra symbols

Outline

DATE:____

TITLE:____

Remember:

Number each new sentence you outline, Use up to 3 words, Use extra symbols

____

____

____

____

____

____

____

____

Outline

DATE:_______________________________________

TITLE:_______________________________________

Remember:

Number each new sentence you outline, Use up to 3 words, Use extra symbols

____

____

____

____

____

____

____

Outline

DATE:____

TITLE:____

Remember:

Number each new sentence you outline, Use up to 3 words, Use extra symbols

____

____

____

____

____

____

____

____

Outline

DATE:_______________________________________

TITLE:_______________________________________

Remember:

Number each new sentence you outline, Use up to 3 words, Use extra symbols

____

____

____

____

____

____

____

____

Outline

DATE:____

TITLE:____

Remember:

Number each new sentence you outline, Use up to 3 words, Use extra symbols

____

____

____

____

____

____

____

____

Outline

DATE:____

TITLE:____

Remember:

Number each new sentence you outline, Use up to 3 words, Use extra symbols

____

____

____

____

____

____

____

____

Outline

DATE:____

TITLE:____

Remember:

Number each new sentence you outline, Use up to 3 words, Use extra symbols

Outline

DATE:____

TITLE:____

Remember:

Number each new sentence you outline, Use up to 3 words, Use extra symbols

____

____

____

____

____

____

____

Outline

DATE:_______________________________________

TITLE:______________________________________

Remember:

Number each new sentence you outline, Use up to 3 words, Use extra symbols

Outline

DATE:____

TITLE:____

Remember:

Number each new sentence you outline, Use up to 3 words, Use extra symbols

Outline

DATE:____

TITLE:____

Remember:

Number each new sentence you outline, Use up to 3 words, Use extra symbols

____

____

____

____

____

____

____

____

Outline

DATE:____

TITLE:_____________________________________

Remember:

Number each new sentence you outline, Use up to 3 words, Use extra symbols

Outline

DATE:_____________________________________

TITLE:_____________________________________

Remember:

Number each new sentence you outline, Use up to 3 words, Use extra symbols

____

____

____

____

____

____

____

____

Outline

DATE:________________________________

TITLE:________________________________

Remember:

Number each new sentence you outline, Use up to 3 words, Use extra symbols

Outline

DATE:____

TITLE:____

Remember:

Number each new sentence you outline, Use up to 3 words, Use extra symbols

____

____

____

____

____

____

____

Outline

DATE:____

TITLE:____

Remember:

Number each new sentence you outline, Use up to 3 words, Use extra symbols

____

____

____

____

____

____

____

Outline

DATE:____

TITLE:____

Remember:

Number each new sentence you outline, Use up to 3 words, Use extra symbols

____

____

____

____

____

____

____

____

Outline

DATE:____

TITLE:____

Remember:

Number each new sentence you outline, Use up to 3 words, Use extra symbols

____

____

____

____

____

____

____

____

Outline

DATE:____

TITLE:____

Remember:

Number each new sentence you outline, Use up to 3 words, Use extra symbols

____

____

____

____

____

____

____

Outline

DATE:________________________________

TITLE:________________________________

Remember:

Number each new sentence you outline, Use up to 3 words, Use extra symbols

____

____

____

____

____

____

____

____

Outline

DATE:_____________________________________

TITLE:____________________________________

Remember:

Number each new sentence you outline, Use up to 3 words, Use extra symbols

Outline

DATE:_________________________________

TITLE:_________________________________

Remember:

Number each new sentence you outline, Use up to 3 words, Use extra symbols

Outline

DATE:_______________________________

TITLE:_______________________________

Remember:

Number each new sentence you outline, Use up to 3 words, Use extra symbols

Outline

DATE:____

TITLE:____

Remember:

Number each new sentence you outline, Use up to 3 words, Use extra symbols

Outline

DATE:____

TITLE:____

Remember:

Number each new sentence you outline, Use up to 3 words, Use extra symbols

Outline

DATE:____

TITLE:____

Remember:

Number each new sentence you outline, Use up to 3 words, Use extra symbols

Outline

DATE:____

TITLE:____

Remember:

Number each new sentence you outline, Use up to 3 words, Use extra symbols

Outline

DATE:_______________________________________

TITLE:_______________________________________

Remember:

Number each new sentence you outline, Use up to 3 words, Use extra symbols

____

____

____

____

____

____

____

____

Outline

DATE:_______________________________________

TITLE:_______________________________________

Remember:

Number each new sentence you outline, Use up to 3 words, Use extra symbols

____

____

____

____

____

____

____

____

Outline

DATE:____

TITLE:____

Remember:

Number each new sentence you outline, Use up to 3 words, Use extra symbols

____

____

____

____

____

____

____

Outline

DATE:_______________________________________

TITLE:______________________________________

Remember:

Number each new sentence you outline, Use up to 3 words, Use extra symbols

____

____

____

____

____

____

____

____

Outline

DATE:____

TITLE:____

Remember:

Number each new sentence you outline, Use up to 3 words, Use extra symbols

____

____

____

____

____

____

____

____

Outline

DATE:____

TITLE:____

Remember:

Number each new sentence you outline, Use up to 3 words, Use extra symbols

____

____

____

____

____

____

____

____

Outline

DATE:____

TITLE:____

Remember:

Number each new sentence you outline, Use up to 3 words, Use extra symbols

____

____

____

____

____

____

____

____

Outline

DATE:____

TITLE:____

Remember:

Number each new sentence you outline, Use up to 3 words, Use extra symbols

____

____

____

____

____

____

____

Outline

DATE:_______________________________________

TITLE:______________________________________

Remember:

Number each new sentence you outline, Use up to 3 words, Use extra symbols

____

____

____

____

____

____

____

____

Outline

DATE:_______________________________________

TITLE:_______________________________________

Remember:

Number each new sentence you outline, Use up to 3 words, Use extra symbols

____

____

____

____

____

____

____

____

Outline

DATE:____

TITLE:____

Remember:

Number each new sentence you outline, Use up to 3 words, Use extra symbols

____

____

____

____

____

____

____

____

Outline

DATE:____

TITLE:____

Remember:

Number each new sentence you outline, Use up to 3 words, Use extra symbols

____

____

____

____

____

____

____

____

Outline

DATE:____

TITLE:____

Remember:

Number each new sentence you outline, Use up to 3 words, Use extra symbols

____

____

____

____

____

____

____

Outline

DATE:____

TITLE:_______________________________________

Remember:

Number each new sentence you outline, Use up to 3 words, Use extra symbols

____

____

____

____

____

____

____

____

Outline

DATE:____

TITLE:____

Remember:

Number each new sentence you outline, Use up to 3 words, Use extra symbols

Outline

DATE:_______________________________________

TITLE:_______________________________________

Remember:

Number each new sentence you outline, Use up to 3 words, Use extra symbols

____

____

____

____

____

____

____

____

Outline

DATE:____

TITLE:____

Remember:

Number each new sentence you outline, Use up to 3 words, Use extra symbols

____

____

____

____

____

____

____

____

Outline

DATE:____

TITLE:____

Remember:

Number each new sentence you outline, Use up to 3 words, Use extra symbols

____

____

____

____

____

____

____

Outline

DATE:_______________________________________

TITLE:______________________________________

Remember:

Number each new sentence you outline, Use up to 3 words, Use extra symbols

Outline

DATE:_______________________________________

TITLE:_______________________________________

Remember:

Number each new sentence you outline, Use up to 3 words, Use extra symbols

____

____

____

____

____

____

____

Outline

DATE:____

TITLE:____

Remember:

Number each new sentence you outline, Use up to 3 words, Use extra symbols

____

____

____

____

____

____

____

____

Outline

DATE:_______________________________________

TITLE:______________________________________

Remember:

Number each new sentence you outline, Use up to 3 words, Use extra symbols

____

____

____

____

____

____

____

____

Outline

DATE:____

TITLE:____

Remember:

Number each new sentence you outline, Use up to 3 words, Use extra symbols

Outline

DATE:_______________________________________

TITLE:______________________________________

Remember:

Number each new sentence you outline, Use up to 3 words, Use extra symbols

Outline

DATE:____

TITLE:____

Remember:

Number each new sentence you outline, Use up to 3 words, Use extra symbols

____

____

____

____

____

____

____

____

Outline

DATE:____

TITLE:____

Remember:

Number each new sentence you outline, Use up to 3 words, Use extra symbols

____

____

____

____

____

____

____

____

Outline

DATE:____

TITLE:____

Remember:

Number each new sentence you outline, Use up to 3 words, Use extra symbols

---

Outline

DATE:____

TITLE:____

Remember:

Number each new sentence you outline, Use up to 3 words, Use extra symbols

Outline

DATE:_______________________________________

TITLE:______________________________________

Remember:

Number each new sentence you outline, Use up to 3 words, Use extra symbols